High Up

Written by Claire Halliday

Series Consultant: Linda Hoyt

WorldWise
Content-based Learning

Contents

Introduction   4

Chapter 1 **The conditions of high-altitude places   6**
Terrain   7
How's the weather up there?   8
Lack of oxygen   9

Chapter 2 **Living high up   10**
Living in the Andes Mountains   12
Living in the Himalayas   16

Chapter 3 **Visiting high-altitude places   20**
High altitude for high performance   22
Modern mountaineers   24

Chapter 4 **Pollution high up   26**
No room at the top   26
Too many tourists?   28
Increasing water pollution   29

Conclusion   30
Glossary   31
Index   32

Introduction

If you ever travel to more than 2,500 metres above sea level, there are particular conditions that would make it hard for you to survive. It's cold and the air is thin. Go high enough, and life becomes very challenging; it becomes too cold to grow food and raise animals.

Yet on land nestled between the world's tallest mountains, some groups of people have adapted to life at high altitude. They have been growing food and raising animals in these places for thousands of years.

Today, more and more people are living in or visiting high-altitude areas. Some high-altitude settlements have grown to "major city status".

What has made this possible and how do people cope with the challenges of these harsh environments?

Chapter 1
The conditions of high-altitude places

High-altitude places have particular conditions that make them unique. The **terrain**, the weather and the lack of oxygen all have an impact on the way people survive.

La Paz, Bolivia, is the highest capital city in the world.

Terrain

The terrain in high-altitude places can be rocky and inhospitable. Mountain peaks surround steep **plateaus** and alpine meadows.

There are three different mountain terrain categories.

Extreme altitude
= above 5,500 metres

Forbidding mountains are the extreme altitude areas closest to the mountain **summit**, where the air is thin and weather conditions are harsh.

Very high altitude
= 3,500–5,500 metres

Rugged mountains are steep, rocky slopes where there is less wildlife. The higher you go in this very high-altitude terrain, the more challenging it becomes.

High altitude
= 2,500–3,500 metres

Alpine meadows are open areas affected by the conditions of high altitude. They are cold and windy, and trees cannot grow there. Alpine meadows are above the tree line but below the permanent snow line. In summer, lush fields of grasses grow there.

How's the weather up there?

Temperature

There are daily weather extremes that see temperatures switch from hot days, with high sunburn danger, to freezing nights.

Altitude has a direct effect on weather. The higher up you go, the more the temperature drops. Generally, the temperature goes down around 2 degrees Celsius for every 300 metres you climb above sea level. Winds are often very strong and the amount of moisture in the atmosphere, known as humidity, is low. This leads to rapid dehydration.

? Did you know?
The summit of Mount Everest is the windiest place on Earth. High-altitude winds have the potential to be a powerful energy source. Scientists believe that if even 1% of the power of high-altitude winds could be harnessed, there would be enough continuous power generated for the world's population.

Wind

Wind blows faster, harder and colder at high altitude. One reason for this is the lack of friction. Objects that are on the earth's surface such as rocks, trees and buildings all slow down the air as it collides with them.

Because the air is much thinner and much lighter at high altitude, it moves at a higher speed.

Snow

At extreme altitudes, snow is constant due to the low temperature. Accumulated snow can suddenly dislodge, particularly during storms, causing dangerous conditions and avalanches.

Lack of oxygen

Because the air is thinner at high altitudes, there is less oxygen for people to breathe. Lack of oxygen can cause serious health problems. It puts stress on our lungs and causes breathing problems. Lack of oxygen is called hypoxia.

Chapter 2

Living high up

Almost 2 per cent of the world's human population lives permanently at high altitude. That's around 140 million people. Some populations of people, especially people who live in the Himalayas and Andes Mountains, have lived there for many thousands of years.

Scientific evidence shows that **hunter-gatherers** were living on the Himalayan peaks more than 20,000 years ago. People began moving into the Andes Mountains more than 11,000 years ago.

Scientists believe that prehistoric people started moving to these areas to find different plant and animal life for food. As climate conditions changed and high-altitude areas became colder and harder to live in, people living there adapted to survive, harvesting the plants and hunting the animals.

Did you know?

People who are born in high-altitude areas have physically adapted and live healthy lives in these extreme conditions.

The Himalayas
8,848 m

Andes Mountains
6,962 m

Rocky Mountains
4,401 m

Farmers at work on the elevated plains of Central Asia

Living in the Andes Mountains

The Andes Mountains stretch from Venezuela right down to the southern tip of the South American continent. They make up the longest north–south mountain range in the world. High **plateaus**, with even higher mountain peaks, make up the landforms. In this mountain range, rivers have carved deep canyons and gorges. The soils are thin, stony and easily eroded.

Mountain life

The Quechua are the largest group of indigenous people in the Andes. Over thousands of years these people have adapted to have different **respiratory systems** from people living at low altitude. They produce extra haemoglobin (red blood cells), which helps them breathe more oxygen.

Most Quechua live on the steep slopes of the mountains where the soil is poor and the weather is cold. Their houses are constructed using local air-dried clay bricks (adobe) or a mixture of tree branches and clay. The roofs are covered with straw, reeds or puna grass.

Did you know?
The Andes mountain range contains the highest peaks in the western hemisphere. The highest is Mount Aconcagua at 6,962 metres above sea level.

The Quechua people survive on subsistence farming, growing enough crops for their own food needs, and some extras to trade for other goods. Their main crop is the native potato, which has adapted to the high-altitude climate and soil conditions. Other cold-tolerant crops include varieties of corn and the grain, quinoa. Small plots of peppers, peanuts and large broad beans are also grown.

Clothing and handicrafts are made from wool spun from llamas, alpacas and guanacos. The wool is woven to make colourful shawls, ponchos and warm caps to wear during the severe winters.

Cows, pigs, chickens and guinea pigs are raised and eaten to add protein to the diet, but this livestock is considered a luxury.

Find out more

The Quechua were part of the famous Incan Empire. Find out more about the structures the Incans built in Machu Picchu, their knowledge of astronomy and how they developed terraces on steep slopes to grow crops of corn and other cereals and grains.

Living in the Andes Mountains

Did you know?

The highest city in the world is La Rinconada in the Andes Mountains, in Peru. At 5,099 metres above sea level, it was initially a gold-mining camp and is now classed as a major city. More than 50,000 people live there.

A city near the clouds

El Alto, with a population of around 1 million people, is one of Bolivia's fastest-growing cities. The city sits at 4,150 metres above sea level on the rim of a canyon. Now the highest major metropolis in the world, its rapid growth is a result of a commercial and construction boom.

El Alto has a cold climate, with the highest average monthly maximum temperature being 17 degrees Celsius in November, and an average of six hours of sunshine each day.

People who live in El Alto have **acclimatised** to living at high altitude, but visitors to the city notice the impact of the high altitude very quickly. It is more difficult to breathe and tourists who are not used to high-altitude living, also notice that it is difficult to sleep and digest food.

Cooking high up also has its challenges. Bakers will see different results from others who cook in low-altitude regions. This is because liquid evaporates faster at high altitude and food dries out more quickly. Even the temperature that water boils at is lower, making cooking basic things like potatoes and rice challenging.

Did you know?

Water boils at 87 degrees Celsius at 3,566 metres above sea level compared to 100 degrees Celsius at sea level.

Living in the Himalayas

The Himalayan ranges form the great mountain system of Asia. Rugged, steep mountain slopes, rocky soil, and the lack of rainfall can make it hard to survive here. People have lived in the Himalayas for generations. Most are involved in their traditional occupation, agriculture.

Over time, these people have adapted to their unique environment. They breathe fast, short, shallow breaths to let their bodies take in more oxygen and they have a higher capacity for exercise than people living at lower altitude.

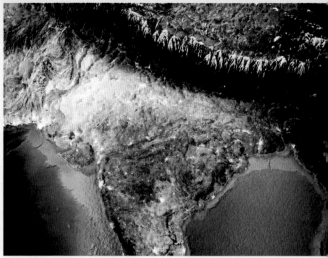

? **Did you know?**

The Himalayas include many of the highest mountains in the world, with Mount Everest being the highest.

The yak

The most important animal in the Himalayas is the yak. Yaks were **domesticated** from wild herds about 3,000 years ago. The only other domesticated animals that can survive at high altitude in these parts are sheep and goats.

It is estimated that about 10 million yaks live on the Central Asian plateau and the Himalayan regions of Nepal, India, Afghanistan and Bhutan.

Most of the people who live in the highland regions are **semi-nomadic** shepherds and yak and horse breeders. In the very cold winter months, they live in huts but on their way to the high pastures over summer, from May to September, they stay in tents or simple houses. During this time, they harvest the new summer grass that has regrown after the winter snow has melted. When they return to their villages with their yaks in autumn, the grass (which is the yaks' only source of food) has dried and is stored for the winter months.

Yaks have adapted to living at high altitude. They have very long hair on their bodies, and a soft undercoat. They can keep warm in the coldest and windiest winter weather and are so well **insulated** that they do not seem bothered when heavy snow builds up on their backs. Yaks can survive when the temperature gets as low as –30 degrees Celsius. They have very thick skins with few sweat glands under their coats so they do not perspire or lose heat from their bodies. To keep their bodies hydrated, they eat snow. In the short, hot summer, yaks shed their hairy coats, which prevents them from overheating.

Yaks produce milk all year. Yak milk is made into butter and cheese.

17

Living in the Himalayas

Sherpas living in Nepal

Sherpas are an **ethnic** group of people from the most mountainous regions in the Himalayas, which includes Mount Everest. They have lived in the region for thousands of years and have physically adapted to the high altitude.

Today, Sherpas are renowned as the guides and **porters** who support and make it possible for climbers to achieve their **summits** on the mountains in the Himalayas. The Sherpas' exceptional climbing skills, superior strength and endurance at high altitudes have made them invaluable to mountaineers.

Sherpas do all the heavy lifting on the mountain, carrying the loads and ferrying supplies to each camp. They may also set up camp and do the risky jobs, such as moving on ahead to position the ropes and ladders for climbers.

Today, high-altitude trekking companies are required by law to provide life and rescue insurance, and medical coverage for Sherpas who work above base camp.

Did you know?

Dal Bhaat is a staple dish in Nepal consisting of white rice alongside curried vegetables and lentil juice. Many Sherpas prefer to eat Dal Bhaat when they are traversing the mountain, as it provides necessary carbohydrates. A carbohydrate-based diet is also important to ensure muscle is not lost.

Mount Everest has a two-month climbing season and the Sherpas need to make multiple trips on the mountain to earn their money. Mountaineering is a dangerous sport and over the years, around one-third of the people who have died while climbing Mount Everest have been Sherpas – casualties of **crevasse** falls, avalanches or altitude sickness.

Climbing Mount Everest is now a business worth millions of dollars. Individuals or teams have to purchase a permit before they are allowed to climb the mountain. Sherpas risk their lives to do the dangerous and physically demanding jobs by supporting the climbing teams on these mountains.

Chapter 3

Visiting high-altitude places

Travellers visiting high-altitude areas need to be aware of the effects high altitude can have on their bodies.

Being at high altitude can cause a loss of appetite, headaches, blurry vision and tiredness. When you suffer lack of oxygen it is hard to think clearly.

For people who are used to living in low altitudes, the impact of high altitude begins to affect them once they reach 1,500 metres above sea level. Above that altitude, the effects are compounded at roughly every 300 metres. This means that the effect of climbing from 1,800 metres to just over 2,000 metres can feel the same as jumping from sea level to high altitude in one quick ascent.

Some people visiting high-altitude areas can get hypoxia. The signs of hypoxia include finding it hard to do simple things, such as climbing stairs or running.

Some signs of hypoxia:
- fatigue
- numbness
- confusion
- blurred vision

Tips to avoid hypoxia:
- ascend slowly
- drink more water
- walk slowly

Climbers at ultra-high altitude need to use oxygen to avoid suffering the effects of hypoxia.

High altitude for high performance

Athletes who compete at high-level endurance sports often train in high altitudes. Fitness experts believe that training in high altitudes makes their bodies stronger.

The reason that many high-performance athletes visit high-altitude regions to train, is because decreased oxygen forces the human body to produce extra red blood cells to deliver oxygen to the muscles. These changes improve their muscle function, giving them more stamina for greater endurance when they return to sea level.

Climbers doing **acclimatisation** training for high-altitude performance on Mount Cook, New Zealand.

When athletes are new to high-altitude training, training specialists must ease them into a training schedule that allows their bodies plenty of time to rest.

One of the best ways to battle altitude sickness is to stay well hydrated. People who train at high-altitude need to increase their fluid intake compared to what they normally drink at lower altitude. How much water do you drink when you play sport?

Modern mountaineers

The biggest challenge for mountaineers is Mount Everest in the Himalayan mountain range in northern Nepal, the world's highest mountain range.

People's ability to survive at high altitude is tested when they attempt to climb high, dangerous mountains but some people want to take on the challenge.

Every year, around 800 people from all over the world attempt to climb Mount Everest. The **crevices**, slippery ice, shifting snow and extreme weather conditions of the rugged **terrain** are dangerous and there are many illnesses associated with high altitude that push the climbers to their limits – both physically and mentally. Many people have died trying to climb the mountain.

Without the right medical care, climbing in high altitudes can be fatal. Most of the climbers who have died on Mount Everest have died in the "death zone". At this altitude, 8,000 metres, there is barely enough oxygen for people to survive and even using bottled oxygen might not help. The causes of death include: being crushed by avalanches, falls, acute mountain sickness, **exposure**, frostbite or freezing to death.

Sir Edmund Hillary and Tenzing Norgay were the first people to reach the summit of Mount Everest on 29 May 1953. Following his successful climb, Sir Edmund Hillary devoted most of his life to helping the Sherpa people of Nepal. He launched a non-profit humanitarian organisation called the Himalayan Trust in the 1960s and with the money that he helped raise, many schools and hospitals were built in Nepal. The Himalayan Trust still operates today and continues to bring quality education, safe water, and better healthcare to communities living in this remote, mountainous region of Nepal.

THE TIMES

EVEREST

COLOUR SUPPLEMENT

LONDON 1953 PRICE 3s. 6d.

COMPANIONS IN ACHIEVEMENT

Sir Edmund Hillary and Tensing Norkey, G.M., who together climbed Everest on Friday, May 29, 1953.

25

Chapter 4

Pollution high up

No room at the top

There are problems associated with the number of people attempting to climb Mount Everest each year. Around 700 climbers and guides spend two months on the mountain. **Human traffic** now chokes the most popular routes to the top of the mountain. Rubbish and human waste continues to grow, and controlling the environmental damage to the once pristine mountain is a challenge.

To reduce the amount of waste on Mount Everest, the Nepali government has ruled that each climber on Mount Everest is required to bring at least 8 kilograms of rubbish off the mountain. Even so, hundreds of kilograms of rubbish are still left behind.

In 2018, the first Mount Everest clean-up campaign was initiated. The campaign focused on items that could be recycled. Most of the waste left on the mountain is empty bottles and cans, empty food tins and discarded mountaineering and trekking equipment. On the first day of the campaign, 1,200 kilogramss of rubbish were airlifted from Lukla airport and flown to Kathmandu for recycling.

Too many tourists?

In Peru, there are problems with too many tourists on the famous high-altitude four-day Inca walking trail that winds through the forests and snow-capped mountains of the Andes Mountains to the historic Incan city of Machu Picchu.

The number of people using the trail is causing erosion. To help reduce the problem, the local government allows only 500 people per day, including **porters**, cooks and guides to walk the trail. There are also strict regulations about not leaving any rubbish (such as snack wrappers, plastic water bottles and paper) behind.

Did you know?

Machu Picchu is around 2,400 metres above sea level.

Increasing water pollution

Lake Titicaca is situated high in the Andes mountain ranges of southern Peru and northern Bolivia. This brilliant blue lake is the largest in South America and is one of the highest navigable lakes in the world. The lake has supported indigenous farming and fishing communities for thousands of years.

Did you know?
Lake Titicaca is 3,800 metres above sea level.

Five major rivers and more than 20 streams feed into Lake Titicaca. Water pollution is an increasing concern for the people who live on the lake. Untreated water waste (including sewage) from surrounding cities ends up in the rivers and streams that flow into the lake. These days, the shores of Lake Titicaca are littered with rubbish and a number of health problems have sprung up among the 1.3 million people who live near its banks.

Conclusion

High-altitude places are difficult environments for all living things. People have adapted to surviving in these places over thousands of years. Over time, they have learned what crops, animals and local materials they require to take care of their basic needs and how to make products and goods that suit their daily lifestyle and customs.

For visitors and tourists, high-altitude places remain potentially dangerous. Special training to help adjust to the specific conditions, combined with a firm knowledge of how to use specialised safety equipment, are essential ingredients to survival in this harsh climate and difficult **terrain**.

Glossary

acclimatised to have become used to a new or different climate

altitude the height of land above the level of the sea

crevasse a very deep, narrow crack found in thick ice

crevices narrow cracks or openings in ice or rocks

domesticated an animal that has been changed from being wild, into one that is kept by people as a pet, on a farm or as a work animal

ethnic people who share common customs, traditions and traits

exposure being unprotected from the cold

human traffic the flow of people moving about in an area

hunter-gatherers people who get most of their food by hunting animals and collecting plants

insulated protected from the cold by a material or covering

plateaus areas of flat land found at high levels

porters people who are paid to carry the bags of tourists or visitors

respiratory system the parts of the body that allow it to breath air

semi-nomadic people who spend a lot of their time moving from place to place following their food source, but who also have places where they live for longer periods of time

summit the highest point of a mountain

terrain the type of features on the surface of the land

Index

alpine meadows 7

Andes Mountains 10, 12, 14

athletes 22, 23

Bolivia 6, 14, 29

cooking 15

dehydration 8

El Alto 14–15

handicrafts 13, 31

haemoglobin 12

Hillary, Sir Edmund 25

Himalayas 10, 16–19, 24, 25

hypoxia 9, 21

Kathmandu 27

Lake Titicaca 29

Machu Picchu 13, 28

Mount Aconcagua 12

Mount Everest 8, 16, 18, 19, 24, 25, 26, 27

Norgay, Tenzing 25

Peru 14, 28, 29

Quechua 12, 13

La Rinconada 14

Sherpa 18–19

snow 7, 9, 17, 24, 28

tourists 15, 28, 30

Venezuela 12

waste 26, 27, 29

wind 7, 8, 9, 17

yaks 17